Graduating with

A Homeschool Diploma

Rebecca Leach

Graduating with
A Homeschool Diploma

How Your Homeschooler Can Graduate With An Official
High School Diploma That Is Accepted (Nearly)
Everywhere

VILLAGE
LANE
PUBLISHING

For Rachel, Elizabeth, Joshua, Bethany, Naomi and Peter.

I had the time of my life fighting dragons with you.

Table of Contents

Introduction

Hello! My name is Rebecca Leach and I am the mother of six children—each of whom graduated with a homeschool high school diploma. I homeschooled my children at different times, in different locations, for the majority of their educations.

When we started my oldest daughter's high school education, I contacted the universities she wanted to attend and was happy to learn that every one of them accepted—in fact, welcomed—homeschool diplomas. I did additional research as we moved to different states and my children wanted to attend different colleges and pursue different career paths. Along the way, I learned a lot about the rules, legalities, and essential points in granting, receiving, attending college and working with homeschool high school diplomas.

Please note that I am not an attorney. Nothing in this book does or is intended to constitute legal advice on homeschooling or any other subject. I am simply a mom who has *been there- done that* with homeschool graduation and diplomas, from the start of high school through standardized tests, college applications, university graduation and launching my adult children into the workforce.

This book is my way of giving back to the homeschool community some of the wonderful things my children and I gained over the years. Homeschooling is at times joyful, frustrating, freeing, fun, and always a learning experience—for parents and kids. Our years of homeschooling in high school were some of our favorite times as a family. The kids were old enough to really dive into their favorite subjects, to get involved in some incredible activities, to pursue their passions, and to engage in deep discussions on all sorts of topics. I wouldn't have missed it for the world.

It is my hope that you and your family will move forward, unafraid of the rumors that circulate about official diplomas, and embrace your homeschooling journey in the high school years.

All the best,

Rebecca Leach

Homeschool Mom

CHAPTER 1

Understanding What a Diploma Is

Bottom Line Up Front:

A diploma is simply a piece of paper issued by someone in authority at a school showing that a student completed a course of study.

M any homeschool parents who sail (or struggle, or both) through the early years of home education find themselves facing something new in the high school years—the question of what to do about graduation, a diploma, getting into college and future career options. I often hear parents sharing all sorts of ideas about homeschooling in elementary and middle school, only to say that they "can't" homeschool for high school.

Many of these parents assume incorrectly that homeschool parents do not have the authority to issue legitimate high school diplomas, or that their students must take accredited classes to graduate. Not wanting to sentence their child to life without a high school diploma, these parents believe they must choose between home schooling for high school or letting their child get a diploma, get into college, and have a successful career. The good news is, both options do coexist.

Homeschool parents can legally issue official high school diplomas.

These diplomas are accepted everywhere in a nearly identical fashion to more traditional diplomas. (The rare exceptions are a small number of city police departments who are resisting legal pressure to acknowledge that homeschool diplomas are official diplomas. See Chapter 4 for more information.)

To better understand homeschool diplomas, how they are issued, who has authority to issue them, where that authority comes from, and what students who graduate from homeschool can do for college and careers, let's begin by examining what, exactly, a diploma is.

What is a Diploma?

The question—*What is a diploma?* —might seem silly at first. We all know what a diploma is, don't we? We can certainly recognize one when we see it. A piece of heavy paper—perhaps parchment—with the school's name across the top in a fancy script, the student's name, some words about what they accomplished, signatures, and perhaps even an official-looking seal of some sort. We honor diplomas. Universities grant acceptance based on them. Employers give promotions because of them. Doctors hang them on their office walls to proudly display the evidence of their years of work and study.

But, what exactly is that fancy piece of paper; where did it come from; and who has authority to issue it? In particular, what exactly is a *high school* diploma?

There are a lot of misconceptions about what a high school diploma is—and what it is not. Let's take a moment to examine what a diploma really is, and in the next chapter we'll look at who has authority to issue official diplomas.

According to Google's dictionary, a *diploma* is

1. A certificate awarded by an educational establishment to show that someone has successfully completed a course of study

2. An official document or charter

Merriam-Webster defines a *diploma* as

1. An official or state document: charter

2. A writing usually under seal conferring some honor or privilege

3. A document bearing record of graduation from or of a degree conferred by an educational institution

Let's take a closer look at these definitions.

A high school diploma is a certificate awarded by an educational establishment (a high school) to show someone has successfully completed a high school course of study. It is a document bearing record of graduation from an educational institution. We will talk more in later chapters about the fact that your homeschool is an "educational establishment," and as a homeschool parent, you are able to decide when a student has completed a course of study. For right now, notice that the actual diploma is a *document* or *certificate*. It is, in effect, a piece of paper.

What makes this piece of paper special? It bears record that someone graduated—or successfully completed a course of study. And it is awarded by an educational establishment. It is official and may be a state document. Finally, it confers some honor or privilege. In the case of a high school diploma, the honors and privileges include being a high school graduate, being eligible to attend college and being qualified for certain jobs.

If you pull out your high school diploma and look at it, you'll see that it includes some specific information: the name of the school you attended, your name, the date you graduated, and signatures of school officials who are vouching for the fact that you actually completed your school's course of study.

There are also some things your diploma does *not* include. It does not include the classes you took in high school, the names of your teachers, or any sort of rating scale for how difficult your school's course of study was.

It is no secret that not all high school courses are created equal. A student graduating from a rigorous college-prep course of study at one school will have a very different education than another student graduating from a school that focuses on technical education or where courses are relatively easy. People know this and expect variations from state to state, city to city, and school to school. Even within one school, two students who

4

select different classes will learn very different things over their years in high school. A high school diploma does not communicate details about a student's education—only that he or she completed the basic requirements for graduation from the school they attended.

Your high school diploma also does not include information on the state or government authority that granted your school permission to educate high school students. Of course, this does not mean your school was operating illegally or unofficially. This is just not information that is included on the diploma.

Diplomas should certainly be official—meaning they should be issued by someone who holds a position of authority at the school whose name is on them. Not just anyone can issue a diploma. As we will see in the next chapter, there are specific ways you, as a homeschool parent, get the authority to issue an official diploma. If someone were to forge a diploma indicating that they graduated from a school they did not attend or did not complete, that would be illegal.

The purpose of this book is not in any way to promote the idea that homeschoolers should issue illegal or fraudulent diplomas. *Quite the contrary!* This book is written to help dispel the many myths that surround homeschool diplomas, including the false idea that homeschool diplomas are in not "real," "official" or "legal."

Homeschool diplomas are, in fact, just as legitimate, official, legal, and widely accepted as traditional diplomas. In the following chapters we will examine who has legal authority to issue official diplomas, what is required for graduation, where homeschool diplomas are recognized and accepted, and how you can legally issue your own children official high school diplomas.

So, to recap, a high school diploma is a certificate or document (a piece of paper) issued by someone in a position of authority at a school, bearing record that the student successfully completed all the requirements to graduate from that school. We also saw that a diploma does not give details about what the student studied, which classes the student completed, or about the legal authority of the school to educate students. This information is found elsewhere.

Now that we have a basic understanding of what a high school diploma is and is not, let's jump right into understanding who has authority to issue high school diplomas, where they get that authority, and how this all applies to homeschoolers.

CHAPTER 2

Who Has Authority to Issue a High School Diploma?

Bottom Line Up Front:

As a homeschool parent, you have legal authority to say when your child has completed their high school course of study, and thus to issue an official, legal high school diploma.

In the last chapter we saw that a high school diploma is a certificate or document showing that a student successfully completed a high school course of study. That leads to the question—who can issue official high school diplomas? And how do they get that authority?

Diplomas are issued by the school that the student is graduating from. If you attend Como Park High School (a public school), your diploma will be issued by Como Park High School. If you attend the private Rabat American School in Rabat, Morocco, your diploma will be issued by the Rabat American School. If you attend American Leadership Academy (a charter school), your diploma will be issued by America Leadership Academy. This might all seem painfully obvious — except that it isn't so clear in many people's minds when it comes to homeschool.

Because of the different definitions of the word *diploma* (see Chapter 1), some people mistakenly assume that in order for a diploma to be official, legal and "real," it must be issued by a state or government. But notice that Como Park High School is not a state or government. Neither is the Rabat American School or the American Leadership Academy. Como Park High school *does* have permission from the state of Minnesota to educate high school students. American Leadership Academy has permission from the state of Utah to educate high school students. The Rabat American School does *not* have permission from any state to educate high school students — but it *does* have permission from the government of Morocco.

So, what about homeschoolers?

In every state in the United States there are laws regarding who can homeschool their children. Homeschooling is legal, when parents follow the homeschool laws for their state, in all 50 states.

So, who has permission from the state to educate *your* high school student?

You do! If you comply with the homeschool laws for your state, *you have official, legal permission from the state to educate your high school student* — just like public, private and charter schools do. This means that you are in charge of a variety of things, including choosing the curriculum your student studies just like public, private and charter schools do, assigning grades just as other schools do, setting graduation requirements just as other schools do, and documenting when your student has successfully completed high school.

Did you catch that?

You have official, legal authority to decide what your homeschool graduation requirements are, and to provide documentation showing that your student completed those requirements—also known as… <u>issuing an official high school diploma</u>.

Where did you get that authority? From the state. When they passed homeschool laws, and when you complied with those laws, they granted you authority to educate your high school student. This includes the legal authority to award high school graduation diplomas.

Remember that a high school diploma is nothing more than a document saying that a student has successfully completed all the requirements for a high school course of study. You, the homeschool parent, set the course of study. And you, the homeschool parent, decide when your student has completed the course of study. When you sign the diploma, you are simply vouching for your student, saying that they completed your school's course of study.

In some states, homeschool parents receive a letter stating that they have met the requirements to homeschool. This letter serves as your official permission from the state to educate your child, including permission to issue official high school diplomas. If your state issues these, KEEP THIS LETTER. Long-term. File it with the same care you would file a birth certificate or a passport. Occasionally universities and employers may ask for a copy of this letter along with your student's diploma and transcript. (More on this later in this book) For now, just remember to keep a copy of this letter in a safe place. If your state does not issue these letters, don't worry about it. You will not be required to provide a letter if you live in a state that does not issue them.

Some people misunderstand *how* official, *how* legal, or *how* real a homeschool high school graduation diploma is.

Homeschool diplomas are exactly as official, legal and real as any other high school diploma.

You (or your husband, neighbor, pastor, mother-in law, or friend) might wonder how this can be. You might argue that this is not "as legitimate" as a public-school diploma, or that your child must take accredited classes for the diploma to be recognized by colleges, universities or future employers. This is not true.

Your student can take whatever classes *you* decide are needed for graduation—in accordance with your state laws. If your state lets parents decide on the curriculum you use to teach your student, then you can decide what courses are needed for graduation.

Accredited classes are not required for graduation.

I graduated from a small private school. The school was a very difficult college-prep school where many of the teachers were former professors from elite universities. However, the school was not accredited for several years. Students graduated and went on to get scholarships to Ivy League and other universities, all without the school or its courses being accredited. This is not uncommon. Many private schools, charter schools, and public schools in the U.S. are not accredited.

Like the students at my high school, homeschool students can get a superior education without ever taking an accredited class. Colleges and universities know this.

A few things to remember:

1. A high school diploma does not give details about the course of study the student completed. It does not say if a student completed a college-prep curriculum, a technical curriculum, or whether they barely passed remedial classes by the skin of their teeth. (I don't recommend this last option for any student — homeschooled or otherwise.) It states only that a student completed a high school course of study.

2. A school — public, private, charter or homeschool — gets permission to issue an official high school diploma when they obtain permission from the state to educate high school students. As a homeschooler who is following the homeschool laws in your state, you have permission to educate your high school students, to say when they have completed their high school education,

and to issue diplomas as evidence to others that they did so.

3. Not all public, private and charter schools in the United States are accredited. Accreditation in the United States falls under the U.S. Secretary of Education and is a requirement for schools *to receive federal funding*. (It is NOT a requirement to graduate students and issue diplomas.) Contrary to popular belief, accreditation is not a gold seal guaranteeing quality education. Homeschoolers do not receive federal funding, so are not regulated or monitored by accreditation boards. Accreditation is not a requirement for a legal high school diploma.

4. Legal authority to issue high school diplomas comes from the state that homeschoolers operate in. When a state passes homeschooling laws and a parent complies with those laws, the parent is granted legal authority to educate high schoolers and to issue high school diplomas.

So, to recap: who has authority to issue official high school diplomas? Any school—public, private, charter or homeschool—that has permission from the state to educate high school students has legal authority from the state to issue a high school diploma. This includes you—the homeschool parent. If your state sends you a letter giving you permission to homeschool, KEEP THIS LETTER. It is your proof down the road that you have authority to issue an official high school diploma. If your state does not issue letters of permission to homeschoolers, you don't need to worry about this.

Now that we understand what diplomas are, and who has authority to issue diplomas, let's take a look at high school graduation requirements.

Rebecca Leach

CHAPTER 3

Graduation Requirements

<u>Bottom Line Up Front:</u>

As the homeschool parent, you decide—in keeping with your state laws—what your graduation requirements are.

G raduation requirements almost always raise questions among homeschool parents. How do you know when your student is "done" with school?

Homeschool education is often different from other types of schooling because school and life overlap in many ways. Family vacation becomes a unit study on beach ecology; a trip to the grocery store includes lessons on budgeting and nutrition; the latest blockbuster movie leads to discussion on character development and plot. How can you ever say, "It's time to be done," when school equals life?

Different states have different requirements for homeschool parents and students, and you should follow your state's laws on what to teach and whether or not standardized testing is required. Some states require that specific subjects be taught—for instance reading, math, social studies and science. Some states require that curriculum be approved, and some require standardized testing. Some states require none of these. Please check your state's current homeschool laws to be sure you are filling their high school requirements.

If you have questions or need clarification on your state's homeschool high school requirements, consider reaching out to your state's department of education. If you are polite and cordial, you will likely find they are helpful and even supportive.

<u>In the end, as long as you follow your state's guidelines, it is likely that *you* can decide to a large extent what your student needs to do to qualify for graduation.</u>

Keeping in mind your state's laws, you might consider one of the following conditions for graduation—or perhaps a mixture of these. I have known families that have used each of these, and many that use a combination.

1. Complete 12 years of attending school, taking the basic subjects, and learning. After 12 years, regardless of what they have learned (hopefully a lot) they are done! This is the most similar to American public schools.

2. Achieve a certain score on the SAT, ACT or another standardized test. Perhaps this is the minimum score needed for a scholarship to their first-choice university. Perhaps it's the national average. I started having my children take the SAT or ACT at least once a year from age 12 on to combat test anxiety and to fulfill a state

requirement that we submit one standardized test score each school year. More on this in Chapter 5.

3. Complete a certain curriculum. If you are using a packaged curriculum, there might be set classes for each grade. When your student completes the classes for 12th grade, they graduate!

4. Reach a certain age. Some parents want their child to stay in high school until they are 16, 17 or 18. At that age, perhaps in May or June, they and their student know that the child will be done with high school. Other parents are happy to let their child finish "early" if they meet the graduation requirements at a younger age. Note that starting college does not have to mean leaving home. There are many excellent online college options that can be completed at home. Most states have mandatory school attendance laws for certain ages. If your student graduates from high school before the mandatory attendance age, they can still attend school by enrolling in and attending college.

5. Complete a pre-determined set of studies or classes. If you are an eclectic homeschooler, you might be pulling together classes from a variety of sources—books, community, online, co-ops, etc. You, your spouse and child might sit down and decide what things you would like your child to know and what classes you would like them to complete in order to graduate. These might include an apprenticeship, life experiences, and other skills and knowledge that are important to you and your family.

6. Some combination of these and other factors. You are the homeschool parent. You are free to be as creative as

you choose with your high school graduation requirements. Just keep in mind your state requirements and make sure you comply with those.

As you can see, graduation requirements can be widely varied! Our family moved often, and my kids occasionally took classes at the local public, private and charter schools. Just like different homeschools have widely different graduation requirements, so do different traditional schools. Some college-prep schools require a number of years of foreign language study. Some rural public schools offer graduation tracks that include tractor repair and cattle-raising. Some charter schools offer cosmetology or CNA licensing as part of their graduation options.

Homeschooling in high school is one of the greatest joys in life. Kids are old enough to really dive into their passions. If you provide latitude for your child to pursue the things they are most interested in, you will find that they often surpass your expectations. Let them learn, dive in, and have fun together!

The important thing is for you, your spouse, and your child to consider ahead of time what skills and knowledge your child will need as they go out into the world, and then to set some requirements for them to achieve those before they graduate. Check your local homeschool laws to make sure you are complying, and then, when your student has filled your requirements — they are ready for graduation!

To recap, just as different traditional schools set different graduation requirements, you, the homeschool parent, set your own graduation requirements. Comply with your state homeschool laws and have fun!

CHAPTER 4

Recognition: What Your Student Can (and Can't) Do with a Homeschool Diploma

Bottom Line Up Front:

A homeschool diploma can do almost anything and everything any other high school diploma can do! The one rare exception is employment with a small number of local police forces.

If you are anything like me as a homeschool parent, you've had more than one night when you woke up in a cold sweat wondering if you were consigning your child to life as a homeless beggar because of homeschooling. (Please tell me I'm not the only one! Yes, I got over it. But there were times!)

Sending your child out into the world with a substandard high school education, unable to get into college or to get a job is not what anyone wants to do.

Let me reassure you right now—having a homeschool diploma will not hold your child back in any way.

Homeschoolers who graduate with homeschool diplomas get into (and graduate with great GPAs from) the top universities in the nation, serve in the military and as police officers, get promotions, serve full-time missions for their churches, and go on to do all the same great things that other high school graduates do. Of course, no diploma guarantees college acceptance or a specific job. But in all 50 states, in private sector jobs, government jobs, state college admissions, private college admissions, and in every other way, homeschool diplomas are accepted everywhere more traditional diplomas are accepted.

I have to add two caveats to this. The first is that there are rare instances of local police forces refusing to accept a homeschool diploma. This is very uncommon, becoming even less common, and is being fought by attorneys who rightly argue that a homeschool diploma is a legal diploma. If your child wants to be a police officer in a specific city, please check with their hiring policies.

You may also occasionally run into individuals who do not understand the legality of homeschool diplomas. This doesn't mean the diploma is not accepted — only that the individual is unaware of the laws.

Because homeschool diplomas are a relatively new thing, there are people who are not aware that homeschool diplomas are legal, official diplomas. This is simply a matter of a lack of understanding on their part, and I encourage you to kindly and cheerfully educate them if you run into someone who doesn't understand homeschool diplomas and who is a gatekeeper to something your student would like to do.

For example, one of my daughters has a disability that allows her to get state funding for help with the things she struggles with. At a meeting one day, a state employee asked my daughter for her high school diploma. When she gave them her diploma with our homeschool name on it, the employee asked where this school was, since she had never heard of it. My daughter explained that she was homeschooled. The employee said she had never heard of this and asked for evidence that homeschool diplomas were legal. I helped my daughter gather and submit our letter from the state saying we had authority to homeschool, and also printed off our state legal code on homeschooling. The employee was impressed and said, "Oh! It looks like you really know what you are doing!" The agency accepted my daughter's diploma and helped her get the assistance she needed.

If your state sends you a letter giving you permission (legal authority) to homeschool, keep it in a safe place. There are a variety of circumstances where you might need to refer someone to it. If your state is one that does not send out letters, don't worry about it. You will not be required to show a letter if your state does not issue them.

Should you need to find your state's legal code on homeschooling, use a search engine to search for "Minnesota Legal Code Homeschool," (substituting your own state's name, of course.) If you have trouble locating it, call your state representative's office or department of education and ask them to point you in the right direction. They are generally very happy to do so.

Getting Into College

Colleges and universities almost always have specific application requirements for homeschoolers. These vary from school to school. Some want a copy of the diploma. Some only require an acceptable SAT or ACT score. Some require a copy of the letter indicating you had permission to homeschool if your state issues such letters. Some want a high school transcript. And some want a combination of these things.

I personally know homeschool students who have attended community colleges, state colleges and universities, private universities, and Ivy League schools with their homeschool diplomas. I have never encountered a college or university that was not welcoming to homeschool students, although some require extra paperwork.

It's a good idea to call the colleges your child is thinking of applying to and speak to an admissions officer in person. You will likely be pleasantly surprised at how happy and welcoming they are to homeschoolers! They can tell you what the requirements are for their school and can help you successfully navigate the application process.

One thing to keep in mind: when you call the admissions office, ask to speak to the admissions officer who works specifically with homeschoolers. Some colleges have all admissions officers work with homeschoolers, while some have a dedicated staff for homeschool applications. If there is a separation, you want to make sure you are speaking with the right person. One of my daughters was given some incorrect information by an admissions officer who was unfamiliar with the school's homeschool policy. In fact, she was initially rejected by her top-pick school—even though we knew their admissions requirements for homeschoolers and she far exceeded them. I called the admissions office and asked to speak to the homeschool admissions officer. When he came on the line and I told him about my daughter's test scores and other criteria and that she had been rejected, he apologized up and down, immediately pulled up her file, reviewed it, and admitted her.

Remember that as the homeschool parent, you are also the college guidance counselor. Never underestimate the power of a phone call!

I talked with one university official who told me their school tracks the performance of their previously-homeschooled students to see how they compare to other students. He said that the homeschoolers as a group out-perform their traditionally-schooled counterparts. Another university admissions officer said, "Homeschoolers are self-motivated and know how to work. I think maybe that's because they grew up learning in an environment that more closely resembles a university than a high school."

For better or for worse, most employers and many universities do not closely examine high school diplomas. When my younger son was applying to a local university, the school asked him to bring in a photocopy of his diploma. Because I was busy, (is any mom not?) and hadn't made his diploma yet, I asked my older son to create the diploma. I asked him to make it "official looking." In my mind, that meant to use typical diploma fonts and formats.

My boys got together to make the diploma and my son printed it off at the university where I met him to sign it. To my horror, as a joke on my asking him to make it look official, my older son had included a large seal on the corner of the diploma with the words "SUPER OFFICIAL" prominently displayed. He thought we would get a good laugh and remove it before printing it and taking it in. But my younger son hadn't even looked at the wording — he just hit print and ran to meet me.

There we were, seated in the admissions office for our appointment, pen in my hand to sign my son's "SUPER OFFICIAL" high school diploma, when they called my son's name. We had no time to fix it. I signed the diploma and handed it him.

Withno more than a quick glance at the diploma, the woman behind the desk took it, stuck it in a file, and handed my son some additional paperwork. We both sighed in relief, and I vowed to look over the diplomas my kids create far enough in advance to fix any spelling errors, typos or "SUPER OFFICIAL" seals.

What would I have done if the woman had said something? I would have explained the joke that my older son had made and offered to bring in a different one if she preferred. Chances are she would have understood and laughed as well. College admissions officers are familiar with homeschoolers.

Serving in the Military or on a Police Force

Occasionally I hear people say that homeschoolers cannot serve in the military or as police officers. This is not true.

The National Defense Authorization Act of 2012 and 2014 removed all barriers to homeschool students serving in the armed forces. According to the Home School Legal Defense Association, in order to enlist in the military, "homeschool graduates will need to have a homeschool high school diploma issued by the graduate's parent or guardian. We strongly recommend that you do not have your homeschool graduate obtain a GED in order to enlist, because the military has almost completely eliminated GED holders from enlisting in the Armed Forces." (HSLDA. Can Homeschoolers Enlist in the Military? https://hslda.org/content/docs/nche/issues/m/military_issue s.asp. Accessed Feb 5, 2019.)

If your child is interested in enlisting in or otherwise joining the armed forces, I strongly recommend visiting the HSLDA page that has guidance for enlistees, currently found here:

https://hslda.org/content/docs/news/2014/201403180.asp

Unlike military service, there is not one national standard for police service. Each individual police organization sets their own requirements for serving. The great majority of police departments and law enforcement training schools accept homeschool diplomas with no issues at all. However, while it is very uncommon, there are still rare instances of police forces discriminating against homeschoolers. These are becoming more and more uncommon, but if your child wants to serve as a police officer, I recommend checking with your local police academy to check on their policy regarding homeschoolers. Most welcome homeschoolers. There are a couple of police academies in the U.S. that do not. If you encounter a problem, consider getting legal assistance to make the academy aware of the legal status of homeschooling in your state.

To recap: The homeschool diploma is just as real as any other high school diploma. With the possible rare exception of discrimination in a few local police departments, your child can do all the same things with a homeschool diploma that they could with a public, private or charter school diploma. Occasionally you might need to provide information to people unfamiliar with homeschooling on homeschool laws and evidence that you complied.

Now that we have covered what your child can do with a homeschool diploma, let's move on to some specific questions parents and others often have about testing and the GED.

CHAPTER 5

Testing—What About the GED, SAT and ACT?

Bottom Line Up Front:

Your student does not need to take the GED because they have a legitimate high school diploma. In some cases, getting a GED may actually hurt them. However, taking the SAT or ACT might be a very good idea—or even necessary.

The GED

B ecause this question comes up so often, let's start by talking about the GED.

GED stands for General Education Development and is a test given to students who dropped out of (or otherwise did not complete) high school. It assesses whether the student has met some basic learning standards generally expected of high school graduates.

Many homeschoolers wonder if they should have their graduating child take the GED, presumably to show that their child learned the basics in high school.

The answer is a *definite NO*.

There is a strong stigma attached to students who take the GED. Because the GED is generally for high school dropouts, people assume—usually rightly so—that an applicant with a GED did not graduate from high school.

Your student *has* a high school diploma. They attended high school, completed all the requirements for graduation, and graduated with an official diploma.

There is absolutely no reason for them to take the GED.

In fact, if your child is considering, or might ever consider enlisting in the military, taking the GED will hurt them. The armed forces accept homeschool diplomas, but they do *not* accept students who have taken the GED.

So, what is a parent to do if they want to provide evidence that their student learned things in high school? Perhaps you, like me, occasionally lie awake in bed at night wondering if you have missed something critical in your child's education. Perhaps your mother-in-law doubts that you are really "doing" school. Perhaps you simply want a way to show anyone who asks that you child did, in fact, learn things all those years they were not getting on the bus in the morning. And perhaps the SAT or ACT are required for admission to the college your child hopes to attend.

One great solution to all these scenarios is to have your child take the SAT or the ACT.

What about the SAT or ACT Tests?

Unlike the GED, there are several reasons it might be a great idea for your student to take the SAT or ACT tests.

First, if your child plans to attend college, it is likely that one of these tests will be required for admission. (See below for discussion of the Accuplacer test that is commonly used at open enrollment and community colleges.) If, as a parent, you want a way to measure your success in teaching—and your child's success in learning high school level material, I strongly recommend signing your child up for one of these national standardized tests.

This is quite simple. You—or they—can sign them up for the test online. (If your child is under a certain age, you might have to walk into a local public-school guidance office to register for the test.) When the registration page asks what school your child attends, there is a registration code or place to indicate your student is homeschooled. If you have trouble locating the code or seeing where to enter this on the registration site, a quick Google search will show you what you need to do. At the time of publication, these tests cost $42-65, depending on which testing options your student chooses.

Students in public school typically take the ACT or SAT during their junior year, but there is no reason younger students cannot take them.

There is no limit on how many times your student can take these tests. Both the SAT and ACT are administered several times a year. Testing locations are at your local public or private high school, generally on Saturday mornings, with options for a different day if Saturday testing poses religious problems. When you register online you will see options for test dates and locations.

As I mentioned earlier, one of the sates we homeschooled in required that we submit a nationally standardized test score for each child annually. At first, I ordered various tests to be sent to our home where I administered them according to the included directions. I'll be honest. This was a real hassle.

At some point, I started looking into SAT and ACT tests and test prep classes for my older kids. I called around and asked about the benefits of enrolling my child in various test prep programs, and I was often told one of the great benefits was that my child could take the test multiple times.

I realized it was MUCH cheaper to order a test prep book for my kids to study at home and sign them up myself to take the test multiple times. From then on, my kids took at least one SAT or ACT test each year from 7th grade through 12th grade. They got lots of testing experience, and since there were no expectations for them to get good scores in 7th grade, the had very little test anxiety.

The College Board—creators of the SAT—now offers two additional PSAT (pre-SAT) tests geared to grades 8/9 or grade 10 for younger students. These are a great option if you want to see how your student compares to national averages for their peers.

Some parents have the mistaken idea that taking the SAT or ACT is only for students who are going to college. While these tests are often (but not always) required for college admissions, they are also useful tools, particularly for homeschoolers.

1. They provide a measuring stick to see how your child compares with national averages in a variety of subject areas.

2. They provide experience taking tests in unfamiliar places. If your child is planning—or thinking they might want to attend college, they will likely be taking tests in testing centers or classrooms. Practice doing this before the "real thing" is invaluable.

3. Taking the test multiple times allows your child to overcome test anxiety related to these tests. When they are in 11th or 12th grade and are taking them for college admissions, they will know how to take the test, have had chances to learn and practice, and will be relaxed and able to perform their best.

Differences Between the SAT and ACT

Overall, the two tests are very similar. They are both accepted by all colleges and universities in the U.S. They both test reading and math, and both have optional writing sections. Both tests strongly emphasize algebra in their math sections.

There are also some key differences. The ACT contains a separate science section while the SAT does not. However, the SAT does test scientific thinking by incorporating scientific passages in the reading, writing and math sections. The ACT math section has more questions on geometry and trigonometry than the SAT. The SAT provides a reference sheet of math formulas, while the ACT does not. Math questions make up ¼ of your score on the ACT while comprising ½ of your score on the SAT — making it twice as important on the SAT.

Should your student choose to take the optional essay writing portion of the tests, there are a few differences as well. On the SAT, the student will be given a passage to read and then asked to dissect the author's argument using logic — not to express their own opinion on the topic. On the ACT, the student is given a passage to read and then asked to analyze the arguments and give their own opinion on the subject.

The ACT is 2 hours 55 minutes without the writing portion and 3 hours 35 minutes with the writing test. The SAT is 3 hours without the essay and 3 hours 50 minutes with the essay. The SAT has a mental math section where students are not allowed to use a calculator, while the ACT allows students to use a calculator on the entire math section. Finally, the SAT gives slightly longer times per question than the ACT.

If your child has a learning disability that has been diagnosed by a doctor, including ADD, you can write to the testing board and request permission for your child to take the SAT or ACT without time limits. You will be asked to provide documentation on the disability. This can be particularly helpful for some students.

What about the Accuplacer?

Many colleges are now asking students who have not taken the SAT or ACT to take the Accuplacer test. This is also administered by the College Board—the creators of the SAT. But unlike the SAT and ACT, it is untimed and is generally administered at the college your student plans to attend. There are remote testing options for students who plan to attend college in a different state.

Unlike the SAT and ACT, the Accuplacer is taken on a computer and scores are available immediately. Colleges use these scores to make recommendations on what math and English classes students should start with—so they can get the help they need if they will benefit from a slower start and so they can bypass courses covering material they already know.

If a student has taken the SAT or ACT, colleges will often use those scores rather than administering the Accuplacer. If you want to know exactly what a college or university requires, give their admissions office a call and they will be happy to explain their school's testing requirements, as well as everything you need to know about the homeschool application process.

Testing Multiple Times

You might be wondering what universities do with a student who has taken the SAT or ACT several times over many years.

The answer is — different things, depending on the school. Some colleges just ask for the most recent score; some want all the scores; some want the individual test with the top score; and some want the top math score, the top reading score, etc. — even if they came from different test dates.

It has never hurt my children (or any other homeschoolers I know) in the college admission process to have taken the test multiple times. It DOES offer parents a way to gauge how their student is doing compared to national averages.

Please keep in mind that these scores are not the end-all and be-all of a child's education. Should you or your child want a higher score for college admissions, tutoring for the tests can be a great help. Test-taking skills need to be taught, just like any other skill, and are necessary for success in college. (Yet another reason to give your kids lots of chances to practice!)

Unlike the GED, taking the SAT or ACT signals to you, your child, and anyone else who may be interested, that your child is receiving a quality high school education.

To recap: Your homeschool graduate does *not* need to take the GED. In fact, doing so may cause people to question the validity of their education and diploma, and will hurt them if they ever decide to enlist in the military.

If you need a standardized test to see for yourself how your student compares to a national average, I recommend the SAT or ACT. You don't need to be planning to attend college to take these tests, but if you do plan to, they are often necessary.

If your student is planning to attend an open enrollment college or university or a community college, they may be asked the take the Accuplacer. Sometimes, SAT and ACT scores will be accepted in place of the Accuplacer.

Now that we have looked at some common standardized testing options that are available for your high school student, and discovered that the GED is definitely *not* a good idea, let's take a look at exactly how to create a beautiful, official high school diploma.

CHAPTER 6

Creating an Official High School Diploma

Bottom Line Up Front:

Like other school administrators, as a homeschool parent you can design and print your own diploma, hire a graphic artist, or order pre-made diplomas to fit your needs.

You now understand the ideas behind homeschool high school diplomas. They are documents showing that your child completed your requirements for graduation. You have the legal authority to issue an official high school diploma to your student when you and your child comply with your state's homeschool laws and your child completes your high school graduation requirements. And you get to decide—following the homeschool laws of your state—what your graduation requirements are.

But, how do you actually design, print and deliver an official high school diploma?

I have designed and printed official diplomas for my own children and for several of my homeschooling friends' children. There is no single right way to design or to print a diploma. However, I have learned a few things over the years about what works best.

When people see a high school diploma, they have certain expectations for what it will look like. As a homeschooler, you are free to be as creative as you like with your diploma. However, because the purpose of issuing a diploma is so the student can show physical proof that they completed high school, I recommend that you follow standard practice in creating a diploma that people will easily recognize as legitimate. (Feel free to create a fire-breathing dragon diploma to frame and hang on the wall if you want, but be sure to also make a more traditional one for the more traditional people your child will encounter in life.)

You have three basic options for creating your child's diploma.

1. Design and print your own diploma

2. Hire a graphic designer and print it yourself

3. Order a custom-made, printed, hard copy diploma

Let's take a look at each of these options individually.

1—Design and Print Your Own Diploma

If you or your child is reasonably comfortable with a computer and you have some very basic graphic design skills, you can easily design and print your own diploma. Start by going to an office supply store and buying a few sheets of high-quality paper, perhaps parchment colored, to print the diploma. You might need a couple of test runs before you get the margins the way you want them. If you want to get really fancy, pick up a gold seal sticker, too. (Don't ask me why, but I swear some people are really impressed with gold stickers on diplomas.)

There are many pre-designed diploma templates available for free online. You can use a search engine to find several options, download, and use one of these. I provide examples to follow later in this chapter. You can also design your own diploma completely from scratch in Microsoft Word or on Canva.com. Personally, I recommend Canva. Canva offers free accounts and has many fun graphic design tools that make creating diplomas and other documents easy. I highly recommend using them.

There is always a question about what to put for the "headline." You can put the words *Homeschool Diploma*, or *Smith Family Homeschool Diploma* (substitute your own family name, of course), *Montclair High school Diploma* (substitute your own homeschool name), or you can simply put *High School Diploma* across the top. Type in your child's name, their graduation date, and make sure you include a place to sign and date the diploma by hand.

Once it's designed, print it off and sign it. Voila! You have an official high school diploma!

2—Hire a Graphic Designer and Print the Diploma Yourself

If you are not confident in your own design or computer skills, you can ask around your friends and family to see if there is someone who loves graphic design and would be interested in creating a diploma for your child. These people may be willing to do it for free, or they might charge a small fee. As I mentioned earlier, I have created many diplomas for my friends. It's fairly quick and I enjoy doing it. Be creative in who you think of to help you. Is there a teenager at your church who is great at making posters? Does your sister make the cutest memes ever for Instagram? Reach out to these people and see if they would be willing to create a diploma for your school.

If you don't know someone with the skills necessary, or you would rather not ask around, check Upwork, Fiverr, and other online markets where people hire graphic designers. Depending on the designer you hire, creating your diploma should cost between $5 and $10. Note that the price does not dictate the quality. Most graphic designers can whip a diploma out in under 10 minutes. Don't pay exorbitant amounts thinking it's necessary to get a quality product.

If you hire someone online, you will probably have to print the diploma yourself. Be sure to ask about printer settings to make sure you can print it and be prepared to print a few test runs to get the margins just how you want them.

3—Buy a Custom-Made Diploma

If you want your child's diploma to be completely created and printed by a professional, there are several options. Online sellers on both Etsy and Amazon will design and print your diploma for you. Working with these designers is similar to hiring a designer on Upwork or Fiverr, except these stores already have diplomas templates created and you simply tell them your school name—or if you want it to just say High School Diploma—and your child's name. Many of them provide the option to mail you a printed diploma. Prices range from approximately $12 to $30.

Now, I can almost hear someone saying, "You have got to be kidding me! You're going to order a high school diploma from Etsy and expect people to take you seriously?"

Yes! Where do you think the local public school gets their diplomas? They design them in house and print them or order them from a designer. You are a school too. You can design your diploma in house or order one from a designer.

For your reference, if you decide to try your hand at designing your own diplomas, here are a couple of common diploma formats to get you started. These designs are both from Canva.com. Should you decide to create your own, I don't know of an easier place to do so. Simply create a free account on Canva, then type Diploma into the search bar. You will see several professional options that you can easily customize and print from home.

Examples:

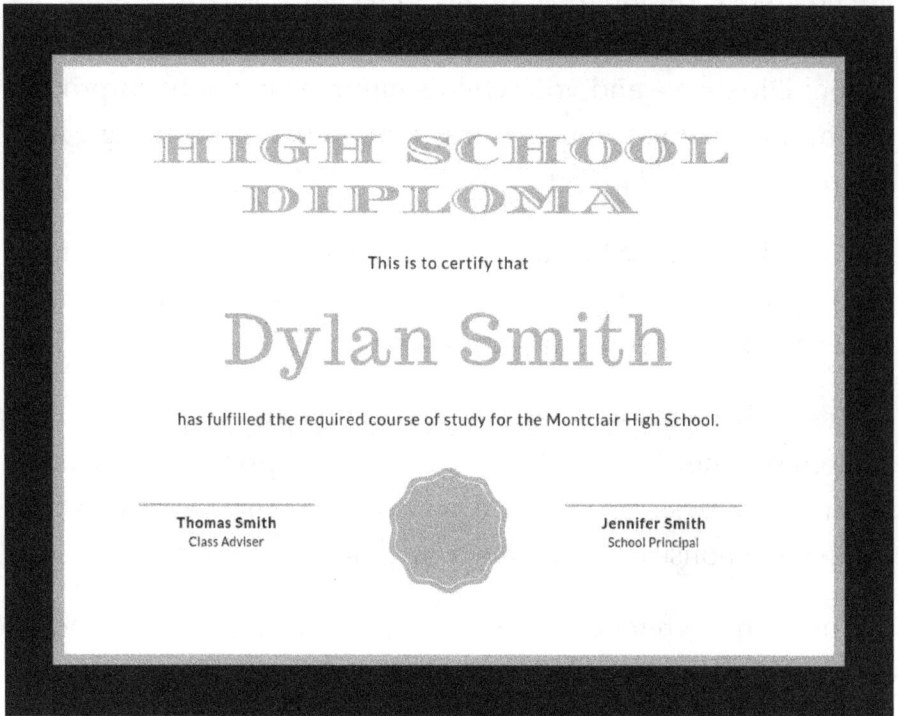

HIGH SCHOOL
DIPLOMA

This is to certify that

Dylan Smith

has fulfilled the required course of study for the Montclair High School.

Thomas Smith
Class Adviser

Jennifer Smith
School Principal

Montclair High School Diploma

Let it be declared that

Miguel Angelo Garcia

has completed all requirements for
High School Graduation.

Kimberly Garcia
School Administrator

Pablo Garcia
School Advisor

So to recap: Like other school administrators, you have several options for how to create and print your student's high school diploma. You can design and print your own, hire a graphic designer to create one that you print, or order one that is pre-made. Whichever option you choose, be sure your diploma is readily recognizable as a diploma.

You are now ready to create your child's diploma! In the next chapter we will go over some final tips and considerations for you and your child in graduating with a homeschool high school diploma.

Rebecca Leach

CHAPTER 7

Final Tips—Filling Out Forms, Creating Transcripts, Assigning Grades, Class Rank and Talking About Your Diploma

<u>Bottom line up front:</u>

When filling out forms, your child should indicate they are a high school graduate, that they were homeschooled or put the name of your homeschool. You can create an official transcript and assign grades. Class rank questions amuse homeschoolers. And the answer to whether your child graduated from high school is simply, "Yes!"

Congratulations! You now have a much better understanding of homeschool high school diplomas than most people.

In this final chapter we'll offer a few tips on filling out forms and applications and discuss how to talk about your student's high school diploma.

Filling Out Forms

There are many times in life when we have to fill out forms about our educational history. These might be for college, for jobs, for standardized tests, and a myriad of other places. When there is a bubble sheet with a question like:

What is your highest level of education? your high school graduate should, of course, indicate that they have graduated from high school.

When your child encounters a form that asks what school they attended, they should enter the name of your homeschool. This might simply be "Homeschool." Or, if you have named your school, it is the name of your school. Our family lived in the town of Montclair for much of our homeschool time, so we called ourselves the Montclair Academy, or Montclair Homeschool. (Sometimes, when we were poking fun at ourselves, we called our school the Montclair Experiment Station School, abbreviated MESS.) If your child does not want to deal with questions about the differences between homeschool and traditional school, you may opt to name you school something that will not make it immediately obvious that you homeschooled. This is simply a matter of privacy. Assuming you are following your local laws, your homeschool is just as legitimate a school as any other school.

As discussed in Chapter 5, the SAT and ACT will both ask your child to indicate what school they are currently attending and both offer the option to indicate homeschool.

Forms also sometimes ask for the location of the school attended. This is simply the city and state where you lived when your child graduated. If they want a street address, use the address where you were living at the time of graduation. The phone number, if required, is your home or cell phone number. In this way, anyone calling with questions about the school can talk to you personally. (I have never heard of anyone calling to check on a homeschool. But, theoretically it could happen.)

What About Transcripts?

As a homeschool parent of a high school student, you should absolutely keep records of what your child studies.

According to the Home School Legal Defense Association, "these records should include your students' attendance records, information on the textbooks and workbooks your student used, samples of your student's schoolwork, correspondence with school officials, portfolios and test results, and any other documents showing that your child is receiving an appropriate education in compliance with the law. You should maintain these records for at least two years. You should keep your student's high school records and proof of compliance with the home education laws during the high school years (including any type of home education notice that you file with state or local officials) on file forever." (HSLDA.org. Feb 5, 2019)

Turning these records into a transcript is very simple.

A transcript is simply a list of the classes a student took, the year they took them, and the grade they received. It is common for colleges and universities to request a copy of students' high school transcripts, so you should be prepared to provide one. They generally want the transcript to be signed by a "school administrator" (homeschool parent.)

When creating your student's transcript, keep in mind all those extra things they were able to do because they were homeschooled. Did they help around the house, cooking dinner and cleaning up after a younger sibling? That can be called *Home Economics*. Did they keep a budget of their expenses and help make financial decisions about their own or family purchases? That could be called *Life Finance and Budgeting*. Did they start a band with their friends and wear out your ears with their electric guitars and drums in the basement? Then add *Music Performance* to their transcript. If they recorded and edited their songs, include *Sound Engineering* in their classes.

These are all things that traditional students do in public, private and charter schools—but there they do them in assigned blocks of time, with a bell to tell them when to start cooking, balancing a checkbook, practicing music, or learning to engineer a song. The fact that your student did these things at various times of the day, in different locations, is simply a function of their being homeschooled.

For the purpose of a transcript, a homeschool "class" is anything your child worked on, spent time on, learned about, practiced, or did. Don't limit yourself to subjects that involved a textbook.

Traditional school transcripts include the school's name, the student's name, the classes taken, grades by semester, trimester, or quarter, the graduation date, and the signature of a school official. Some colleges also want a short description of each class that is listed. You can include all these things yourself.

Assigning Grades

Perhaps you are wondering what to do about assigning grades. Some homeschool parents follow a school pattern similar to public schools, perhaps with someone other than the parent assigning grades — especially if the student is enrolled in an online school or other form of distance education. If this is the case, then you may be able to request a transcript — and even a diploma — from the distance education institution. If you are issuing the diploma yourself, feel free to add other things to the transcript that your child has done, like scouts, music, etc. to round out the picture of their high school years.

If you are the teacher, then you get to assign the grades. Be fair and realistic. If your child really struggled through algebra, don't give him an A. On the other hand, recognize that even in traditional schools, grades are not completely objective. Teachers get to know their students and often reward extra effort with higher grades when they can see that the student really gave it their all.

To help you in creating your student's transcript, I've included two sample formats at the end of this chapter. Both were created in Microsoft Word, the second using a template. You do not need to do anything fancy. In fact, most transcripts are rather bland, with very little attention paid to graphic design.

What About Class Rank?

This is a particularly funny question for homeschoolers. Unless your child is a twin, triplet or other multiple, they are literally in a class of their own. They are simultaneously top in their class, at the 50th percentile, and the bottom in their class. No one who understands homeschooling will ask about your student's class rank.

However, this question occasionally comes up on college applications. If your child has to put an answer, let them indicate that they are at the top of their class. Why? Because if a computer is the only thing looking at this, it won't make a huge difference—other than to get your student's application processed and handed to a live person to make a final decision.

Once a real person looks over your child's application, they will see that your child was homeschooled, and they will understand the class rank question for what it is—a non-question with a non-answer. They will understand that your child had to mark something and will either ignore it completely or smile at the response.

How to Talk About Your Student's Diploma

The last topic we will discuss is how you and your child should talk about your child's high school diploma.

Neither you nor your child ever needs to apologize for—or qualify—your child's diploma. When someone asks, "Did you graduate from high school?" the answer is "Yes!" When someone asks, "Do you have a high school diploma?" the answer is "Yes!"

I occasionally hear a homeschooler answer the question "Did you graduate from high school?" with something along the lines of, "Well, I was homeschooled..." or worse— "No, I was homeschooled." Can you imagine someone asking if you graduated from high school, and answering, "Well, I went to my local public school..."

Umm... Does that somehow mean you only sort of graduated?

(As a side note, someday I would love to hear a variation on a common question. Rather than, "Why did you decide to homeschool?" I would love to hear, "Your kids are in public school? Interesting. What made you decide to public school?")

When homeschoolers answer these graduation questions in non-committal ways, they send a message that homeschooling is not *really* school. We all know that homeschooling is different from traditional school—that is presumably why you are homeschooling in the first place! But it is not inferior. Remember that one traditional school can be starkly different from another traditional school, and that does not mean one of them is inferior. And a homeschool diploma is not inferior either. There is no need to qualify, explain, or negate your child's diploma.

Is your child a high school graduate with a diploma?

Yes!

They absolutely are.

End of discussion.

If someone questions the legitimacy of the diploma, be prepared to offer information—verbal or in writing as appropriate—about homeschool laws in your area. Let them know that homeschooling is a legal and official way to attend and graduate from school, just as public, private and charter schools are different options. Share this with a smile and self-confidence. You are a school administrator, a teacher, and a parent all rolled into one. If anyone understands education, it's you!

Official High School Transcript
Chesapeake Bay Academy
Woodbridge VA 22025
(555) 123-4567

Jill M. Peterson

9th Grade   2006-2007

	Semester 1	Semester 2
American Literature	A-	A
Algebra I	B+	B-
Ancient Roman History	C	C+
Earth Science	A	B+
Latin I	A	A
French I	B-	C+
Drama	A	A
JROTC	B	B+
Music Production	A	A
Girl Scouts	A	A

10th Grade   2007-2008

	Semester 1	Semester 2
English Literature	A	A-
Geometry	A	A
World History	A-	A
Biology	C+	C

53

Latin II	A-	A-
French II	B+	B
Advanced Drama	A	A
JROTC	A-	B+
Music Production	A	A
Film Production	A	A
Girl Scouts	A	A

11th Grade   2008-2009

	Semester 1	Semester 2
Mythology in Classical Literature	A-	A
Algebra II	B	B-
Art of Roman Warfare	A	A-
Chemistry	B-	C
Latin III	A	A-
Advanced Drama II	A	A
Advanced Music Production	A	A
Advanced Film Production	A	A
Intro to Auto Mechanics	A	A-

12th Grade   2009-2010

	Semester 1	Semester 2
Composition and Research Writing	A-	A-

Trig and Pre-Calculus	B+	B-
Classical Philosophy & Logic	A	A
Art of Greek Warfare	A	A
Physics	A-	A
Latin IV	A	A-
Advanced Drama III	A	A
Advanced Music Production	A	A
Advanced Film Production	A	A
Internship—Jamestown Historic Ships	B+	B+

A H   APOLO HOMESCHOOL
JOHN A. SMITH

GRADUATION

June 15, 2016

Cumulative GPA:
3.6

Honors:
Eagle Scout
Shakespeare Festival:
Sweepstakes Winner
First Place, One Act

JOHN A. SMITH

APOLO HOMESCHOOL, ST. PAUL MINNESOTA

9TH GRADE

9th Grade English	A	A
American classic literature, including essay writing and journal keeping		
9th Grade Math	C-	B-
Topics in Algebra I, introductory Geometry, life math		
Environmental Science	A-	A
Utah geography and environment, natural plants and wildlife		
US History	A	A
Constitution, Declaration of Independence, political science		
Wilderness Survival	B+	A
250+ miles backpacking, water purification, food identification		
Psychology	C-	A-
PTSD, human interaction, addiction cycle, healthy life management		
Home Economics	B	B+
Cooking and home repair		

10th Grade

10th Grade English	A-	B+
British Literature, essay writing, and journal keeping		
10th Grade Math	B-	B
Topics in Algebra I, Geometry, and life math		
Astronomy	A	B+
Planets, solar system, Goldilocks Zone, red shift		
Social Science	A	A
Forms of government- US and foreign, Economics		
Latin I	B-	B
Vocabulary, verb conjugation and basic sentence structure		
Ballroom Dance	A	A
Salsa, Square dance, jazz, swing dance		
Theatre and Film	A	A
Sitcom, red curtain, Broadway, and silent film		

11th Grade

Course		
Honors Literature	B	B-
Social construct, government and personal freedom in great literature		
Secondary Mathematics II	B+	B
Topics in Algebra II, Geometry and Trig		
Computer Programming I	A	A
JAVA, binary code, game design		
World Civilization	C-	B-
Byzantine Empire to modern era		
Advanced Drama Practicum IV	A	A-
Produced and Performed Shakespeare and contemporary, monologue		
American Sign Language I	B-	B
ASL language, deaf culture and history		
TV Broadcasting	A	A
Produced daily news broadcasts		

12th Grade

Course		
Advanced Language Arts	B-	A
Dystopian societies, US Constitution, communism, religious freedom		
Secondary Mathematics III	C	B-
Topics in Algebra II, Geometry and Trig		
Physics	B-	B
Newtonian physics, astrophysics, and quantum mechanics		
Computer Technology	A	A
Certifications in MS Word, PowerPoint, Excel and more		
Robotics and Automation	A	A
Artificial Intelligence, legal code and ethics		
Improvisational Theatre	A	A
Principles of improv and performance		
Advanced Cooking	A	A
Cultural food, safety, and cooking techniques		
American Sign Language II	B	A-
ASL language, deaf culture and history		

_____   _____
Chesapeake Bay Homeschool Principal   Date

Conclusion

There you have it! You are now ready to embark on your homeschool high school adventure. You are armed with information on what a diploma is, who has authority to issue a diploma and where they get that authority. You understand that when you comply with your state's homeschool laws, you have authority from your state to issue an official high school diploma. You have seen that as a homeschool parent, you are responsible for setting your own graduation requirements in keeping with your state laws. You now know that your child can do just about everything and anything (with the possible exception working for a few local police forces) with their homeschool diploma that any public or private school graduate can do. You understand the benefits of signing your child up for the SAT or ACT, and you know that they should not take the GED as this can actually hurt their employment opportunities, especially with the military. You have seen how to create an actual diploma yourself or hire a graphic designer to create one for you. And finally, you know how to talk to others about your child's diploma with confidence and authority.

That is a lot of information you have taken in. Good job!

Please take the opportunity as it arises to share this information with others—through word of mouth or online through social media. Pass along or recommend this book to other homeschool parents. Write a review on Goodreads or Amazon. The more that homeschoolers and the general public understand the legitimacy of homeschool diplomas, the easier it will be for our children to talk about their diplomas and school experiences without lengthy explanations, and the more homeschooling in general will be embraced.

It is my hope that you will delight in spending your child's high school years together, learning and growing and becoming your best selves.

May your journey be full of joy!